The Saints

At War

by

Frank D. Hammond

ORDER FROM:
LAKE HAMILTON BIBLE CAMP
P. O. BOX 21516
HOT SPRINGS, AR 71903
(501) 525-8204
www.lakehamiltonbiblecamp.com

The Saints At War, by Frank D. Hammond
ISBN # 0-89228-104-9

Revised Edition Copyright ©, 1997
Impact Christian Books, Inc.
332 Leffingwell, Suite 101,
Kirkwood, Mo. 63122

Original Copyright ©, 1986, by Frank D. Hammond

Cover design: David Pitts

Printed in the United States of America

CONTENTS

Foreword

Truth is the key to freedom. Jesus said, *You will know the truth, and the truth will set you free* (John 8:32). There is much truth in the Bible which pertains to Satan and his kingdom. This area of biblical truth is a necessary part of that which must be embraced in order to experience freedom. It is certainly a fact that Jesus spent much of His earthly ministry in dealing with the devil and in emphasizing principles of spiritual warfare. If it were not important for us to know about Satan and his ways then the Bible would have remained silent on the subject. Satan is the one who stands to lose the most when Christians gain understanding about him. No wonder the arch deceiver tries to discourage any investigation of his person and his works.

Satan does not want us to understand that he has already been defeated. Jesus defeated the devil. He took away all the armor in which Satan trusted. (See: Luke 11:22.) Therefore, the devil can do no more than we permit him to do. When Christians really comprehend Satan's limitations and their own equipping, they will be encouraged to confront the devil directly, bind him and spoil his house.

There are two levels of spiritual warfare. One level of warfare involves the casting out of demons. This is commonly designated as the ministry of deliverance. A second level of warfare is that of wrestling against principalities, powers, world rulers and spirits of wickedness in the heavenlies. (See: Ephesians 6:12).

v

It is time for the Church to confront these spiritual Goliaths. You may recall that young David conquered the giant with his slingshot, but he became experienced with his weapon while protecting his sheep from lions and bears.

In a similar way, the Church has been learning the tactics of spiritual warfare through deliverance ministry among the "sheep," and now it is time to face demonic strong men.

This book has been written because of a deep desire of heart that the Church, God's army, become totally aggressive in spiritual warfare. Too many Christian soldiers remain inactive and ineffective in the time of battle. It is my prayer that all the saints of God will become *saints at war*!

Frank Hammond

I

The Authority of the Believer

Ephesians 1:18-2:6

An unseen war is raging on every front: the war between the forces of righteousness and the forces of wickedness and between God and Satan. The world, the nation, the Church, the family and every individual on planet earth are specific targets of attack by *the spiritual forces of evil in the heavenly realms* (Ephesians 6:12). The average man on the street is totally unaware of the invisible war, even though he is very directly involved, and in many cases he is being swept away by the forces arrayed against him. He interprets everything from world crises to personal traumas as natural happenings. He sees no connection between unseen spiritual forces and such life tragedies as divorce, illegitimacy, sexual perversion, abortion, child abuse, disease, financial collapse, drug abuse and crime. Furthermore, Mr. Average Citizen believes that man is his own savior, and that increased knowledge and scientific advancement will eventually remedy all of mankind's problems.

While the forces of evil have been increasing in boldness and strength, even to the point of seeming invincibility, our God has been gathering and training a vast army of spiritual soldiers. These soldiers of the Cross know who the enemy is, and are not ignorant of his tactics. They know their spiritual weapons and how to bind the satanic strong men. The trumpet of God is now sounding the call to battle. It is time for His great army to go forth in full battle array. This army is the true Church of the Living God. (Not everything that is called "church" is *His* Church.) Time is running out. Arise, O Church!

We Must Be Spiritually Aware

The Army of God that is now in the forefront of the battle is a mere remnant of the total Church. God has always worked through remnants and used the weak to confound the mighty. Yet, the invitation remains open for others to fill the ranks. Christian, are you truly aware of the intensifying battle? Have you recognized God's call to active duty? Do you understand the spiritual power made available to you?

Are there evil things happening around you which threaten your peace, the unity of your family, the blessings of freedom, and the future of your nation? Do you know that you have the power in God to overthrow the kingdom of Satan and to establish the Kingdom of God? Do you know who you really are as God's child? Do you know the spiritual authority that you possess and the source of it? Has this authority remained unused, allowing the powers of satanic darkness to roll unchallenged across the land? Do you know that Christ has given His Church both the responsibility and the ability to change the course of history? Do you know that the salvation of our nation, the Church itself, the family and freedom can only be assured through spiritual warfare?

Our struggle is not against flesh and blood (Ephesians 6:12); therefore, *The weapons we fight with are not the*

8

weapons of the world (II Corinthians 10:4). This clearly means that victory will not come through social reform, education, political action or fleshly confrontation. The battle is not on the earth and not against flesh and blood. The battle is in the heavenlies; it is an assault against Satan's command post.

We Must Know Our Spiritual Position

The Apostle Paul prayed earnestly for the churches with whom he was related. If he were alive today, he would undoubtedly pray the same forceful prayers for the churches today that he prayed centuries ago. He found the Church ignorant of her spiritual position in Christ and of her spiritual authority over the kingdom of Satan.

> *I pray also that the eyes of your heart may be enlightened in order that you may know...his incomparable great power for us who believe. That power is like the working of his mighty strength, which he exerted in Christ when he raised him from the dead and seated him at his right hand in the heavenly realms.* (Ephesians 1:18-20)

Saints, God yearns that we become aware of the incomparable great power which we now possess. What is the source of our power? It is the same power by which Christ was raised from the dead. Think of it! The power of resurrection life is in us! The very same Spirit which raised Christ from the dead is resident in each Christian believer. The indwelling Holy Spirit gives the believer the ability to do the mighty works of God.

The believer in Christ has not only the spiritual ability of the Holy Spirit in him, but also the authority of the name of Jesus. This is the authority to rule and reign, even as Christ now rules and reigns from the throne of God in the heavenly realms. The throne of God represents kingship. Jesus is King: He is Lord of all. Furthermore, Jesus said, *All authority in heaven and on earth has been given unto me. Therefore go...* (Matthew 28:18). That is, He gave His disciples commission to go into all the world with the message of His Kingdom, and the right to go in His authority. To go in His name means to go in His authority. We have a spiritual power of attorney: the legal right to act in behalf of Another. The name "Jesus" is the name of absolute authority. It is the name by which a new believer is baptized in water, and it is the name by which demons are cast out and the kingdom of Satan overthrown. God wants us to know with absolute assurance that we have power and authority, and He wants us to know The Source.

What is the scope of Christ's power and authority which has been made available to us? It is:

Far above all rule and authority, power and dominion, and every title that can be given, not only in the present age but also in the one to come.
(Ephesians 1:21)

The power and authority of our Christ is above ALL other rule and dominion, and this specifically includes the rule of Satan and all of his demons. The devil will never prevail against Christ or His Church, for Christ's absolute lordship extends throughout this age and the age to come.

Christ has allowed Satan to act out his rebellion to the full, in order that the folly of his pride will be clearly evidenced forever as an example to all of God's created beings. However, God has set a time to end Satan's rule, and has decreed that His Church will be His instrument to bring about the end of the rebel's reign of destruction. There are many reasons to believe that Satan's time of overthrow is at hand. When the whole world stands on the brink of destruction, can the fullness of God's Kingdom on earth be far away? Why else has God chosen this generation of the Church to confront the powers of this dark world and the spiritual forces of evil in the heavenly realms?

Satan Underfoot

And God placed all things under his feet and appointed him to be head over everything for the church, which is his body, the fullness of him who fills everything in every way.
(Ephesians 1:22-23)

The Church is His very body, and He is the Head. What Christ is, the Church is, in Him. Since Christ has the devil under His feet, then the Church also has the devil under her feet.

It must not go unnoticed that the position of both Christ's throne and Satan's headquarters are *in the heavenly realms* (compare: Ephesians 1:20; 6:12). We must recognize that the "heavens" or "heavenly realms" represent three distinct areas. Paul speaks of being caught up to the third heaven (II Corinthians 12:2). If there is a third heaven, there must also be a first and a second. We can consider the first heaven as the atmosphere around the earth. The second heaven is above the first, and it is the heavenly sphere in which Satan, *the prince of the power of the air* (Ephesians 2:2), has his domain. The third heaven is the place of God's abode.

Now we are told:

And God raised us up with Christ and seated us with him
in the heavenly realms in Christ Jesus.

(Ephesians 2:6)

This is a clear declaration that we, the believers, are seated with Christ in His throne. The second heaven is under us and has become our footstool, which speaks of subjugation. We have the exact same authority over the devil that Christ has. Since Christ is the Head of the Church, and the Church is His body, then it follows that the Church has the devil underfoot (see: Hebrews 2:5-9).

Believer, you were not always in this enviable position. Here is a picture of your condition before you knew Him:

As for you, you were dead in your transgressions and sins,
in which you used to live when you followed the ways of
this world and of the ruler of the kingdom of the air, the
spirit who is now at work in those who are disobedient.

(Ephesians 2:1-2)

Then, by God's grace you were saved, made alive and raised up with Christ and enthroned with Him in His heavenly realm. You are somebody in Christ. You are seated on the throne of God in power. This promise is not speaking of future glory, but of your present position. Lay hold of this truth.

Too many Christians do not believe enough concerning their power and authority. The devil has deceived them into thinking that they are nobodies without any ability to change anything that he is doing. Before we enter the arena of conquest against the devil, the final conflict between him and the Church, we MUST know who we are in Christ and know the spiritual power and authority invested in us by Christ.

The reason that we can have power over all the power of the devil is that we are seated with Christ in His throne. We have the same power over the satanic principalities and powers in the heavenlies that we have over demons indwelling an individual. Right now, make this positive confession about yourself on the basis of what the Word of God says about you:

I am God's child, redeemed by the blood of Jesus. I am a partaker in the benefits of Christ's death and resurrection. He has given me His eternal life and God has raised me up with Christ and seated me together with Christ upon His throne in the heavenlies. He has given me a position of authority over all the power of the devil. I have spiritual dominion. The devil is under my feet. Amen.

Christ and His Church

Psalm 110

This great Psalm gives us even further insight into Christ's dominion over Satan which is shared by His Church. The Psalm is prophetic.

The Lord says to my Lord: sit at my right hand until I make your enemies a footstool for your feet.
(Psalm 110:1)

In the Spirit, David hears the Father speak to the Son, inviting Him to sit at His right hand until all of His enemies are made a footstool for His feet. The sons of God now share that throne with the Son of God. Our Lord has given

His Church the commission to assault the very gates of Hades. As the Church puts Satan under her feet, he will be put under Christ's feet. Believer, exercise your authority in Christ over the principalities and powers of Satan and, *The God of peace will soon crush Satan under your feet* (Romans 16:20).

> *The Lord will extend your mighty scepter from Zion; you will rule in the midst of your enemies.*
>   (Psalm 110:2)

"Zion" speaks prophetically of the Church. The scepter represents authority. Christ's Church will become an extension of His authority and will rule in the midst of His enemies. Today God's people are surrounded by spiritual enemies. Let the Church take up the scepter of spiritual authority and rule for Jesus' sake.

This prophetic Psalm assures us that the Church will exercise her ability in spiritual battle.

> *Your troops will be willing on your day of battle. Arrayed in holy majesty, from the womb of the dawn you will receive the dew of your youth.* (Psalm 110:3)

Around the world today the army of God is rising to battle. The emerging of God's army is being witnessed in country after country. There is a battle cry resounding in our world like that of Gideon and his men: *A sword for the Lord and for Gideon* (Judges 7:20). Gideon's men were a willing band in the day for battle. Their faces were set, and their hearts were undivided. As each man kept his assignment, there was victory: *While each man held his position around the camp, all the Midianites ran, crying out as they fled* (Judges 7:21).

14

This army is dressed in holy array: the whole armor of God. Each soldier has girded himself with truth, put on the breastplate of righteousness, shod his feet with readiness to wage peace, taken up the shield of faith, protected his head with the helmet of salvation, lifted up the Sword of the Spirit, which is God's Word, and is daily engaged in fervent prayer (see Ephesians 6:10-18]. This army is as fresh as the dew and as strong as the youth. What shall the Lord accomplish through His army?

The Lord is at your right hand; he will crush kings on the day of his wrath...crushing the rulers of the whole earth.
(Psalm 110:5-6)

These kings and rulers of the world have already been identified for us in Ephesians 6:12 as the rulers, authorities, powers of this dark world and the spiritual forces of evil **in the heavenlies**. These satanic rulers in the air work through earthly rulers; and they, rather than human rulers, are the unseen powers against whom the Church launches its attack. They are the rulers within Satan's kingdom who have been set over nations and cities around the world. Under the leadership of King Jesus, the potentates in the heavenlies are crushed.

Let the saints rejoice in this honor and sing for joy on their beds. May the praise of God be in their mouths and a double-edged sword in their hands, to inflict vengeance on the nations and punishment on the peoples, to bind their kings with fetters, their nobles with shackles of iron, to carry out the sentence written against them. This is the glory of all his saints. Praise the Lord.
(Psalm 149:5-9)

II

Binding the Strong Man

Matthew 12:22-33

Then they brought him a demon-possessed man who was blind and mute, and Jesus healed him, so that he could both talk and see.   (Matthew 12:22)

In the context of Matthew chapter 12 Jesus is involved in deliverance ministry. That is, He is casting out demons. A man is brought to Jesus whom demons have made both blind and mute. The man's condition is typical of Satan's evil work in the lives of those whom he enslaves. Without fanfare Jesus simply "healed" the man by casting out the afflicting spirit(s).

By What Authority?

The work of Satan and that of Jesus are brought into contrast. Satan had put the man into bondage, and Jesus came to deliver him from his bondage. The onlookers were divided in their opinion as to the authority by which Jesus performed this miracle of deliverance. Some thought He was the Christ and others thought he was the devil, himself.

All the people were astonished and said. 'Could this be the Son of David?' But when the Pharisees heard this, they said, 'It is only by Beelzebub, the prince of demons, that this fellow drives out demons.'   (Matthew 12:23-24)

When Jesus perceived their thoughts concerning Him, He began to openly answer them by showing how illogical they were in their thinking.

Jesus knew their thoughts and said to them. 'Every kingdom divided against itself will be ruined, and every city or household divided against itself will not stand. If Satan drives out Satan, he is divided against himself. How then can his kingdom stand?'

(Matthew 12:25-26)

Jesus recognized the existence of Satan's kingdom. Satan is a ruler, and he has a kingdom. But the Kingdom of God is greater in power than that of Satan. This is why Jesus, the Ruler who has all power and authority, was able to undo the work of His adversary.

Jesus declared that Satan's kingdom is not divided. We can be assured that it is not kept in unity by a loyalty of love, for there is no love in the demonic realm. Rather, Satan's minion's are tenaciously bound together by their common goal of evil and the fear of their master. Truly, Satan's kingdom is not divided. Neither is Satan involved in true deliverance. He is only interested in introducing demons into men's lives, not in casting them out. Otherwise, his kingdom would soon self-destruct.

By what power, then, did Jesus deliver this man? And what is the significance of such a deliverance?

But if I drive out demons by the Spirit of God, then the kingdom of God has come upon you.

(Matthew 12:28)

Jesus had defeated Satan by the power of "the Spirit of God." This was evidence, to those who would accept it, that the Kingdom of God had come in the power and love of deliverance. Each time a deliverance takes place, it is continuing evidence that the Kingdom of God is greater than that of Satan. Too, each encounter with a demon spirit is an encounter with the whole satanic kingdom. Since the kingdom of Satan is not divided, it can be said to be joined together. Like the private in the army is linked to the commanding general through a chain of command, the lowliest demon in Satan's ranks is connected to Satan himself and to all other spirits in that kingdom by a similar chain of authority. It then follows that each deliverance victory is a partial victory over Satan's kingdom. A blow against one demon is a blow against the whole kingdom of Satan.

The Spiritual Principle

Or, again, how can anyone enter a strong man's house and carry off his possessions unless he first ties up the strong man? Then he can rob his house.
(Matthew 12:29)

This is the key verse in the passage. In answer to the queries of His critics, Jesus reveals the secret of His success. He has already told them that His power of ministry was *the Spirit of God*. Now, He further explains that this power was used to *tie up the strong man*. The familiar language of the King James translation reads: *bind the strong man*.

Binding the strong man is a basic principle of spiritual warfare. Before any spiritual victory can be won against Satan, the strong man must first be bound. This is true whether the arena of warfare is the life of an individual, a family, a city or a nation. In the case of the blind mute, the devil's possession was the unfortunate man. Once the strong man was bound, Jesus entered freely into his house and carried off Satan's possession. In simple language, the man was delivered, and Satan had no more control over his body.

In Chapter IV we will explore the important matter of binding and loosing as a principle of spiritual warfare.

III

Spoiling The Strong Man

From Matthew 12:29 we discover that binding the strong man is the prelude to spoiling his house:

Or, again, how can anyone enter a strong man's house and carry off his possessions unless he first ties up the strong man? Then he can rob his house.
                                                    (Matthew 12:29)

This verse gives us the key to successful spiritual warfare. It behooves us to study the verse carefully. In pursuit of a deeper understanding of "first bind the strong man," let us consider key words in the passage.

The Strong Man

The strong man must first be bound. Of whom is Jesus speaking? He is speaking of Satan. Satan is the strong man who opposes Christ, His Church and His people. So, *the strong man* is Satan, OR anyone to whom Satan has delegated authority. Satan is the head of a demonic kingdom, and much of his work is carried out by delegated authority. Jesus recognized the existence of Satan's kingdom in Matthew 12:25,26. The kingdom over which the devil rules is "not divided." That is, the devil is not in the deliverance ministry. If he were casting out demons then he would be divided against himself and would soon self-destruct.

21

Every kingdom has structure, organization and authority. In the Kingdom of God, Jesus is the Supreme Authority. He declared, *All authority is given unto me in heaven and in earth* (Matthew 28:19). All authority is vested in Jesus Christ, yet He has chosen to delegate authority to others. For example, he has delegated authority to the husband in the family. The husband has been made *head of the wife, even as Christ is the head of the church* (Ephesians 5:23). Also, Christ has delegated authority in the church. Therefore, we are admonished, *Obey your leaders and submit to their authority. They keep watch over you as men who must give an account* (Hebrews 13:17). Even those who rule over nations are acting under delegated authority from Christ (see Romans 13: 1-7).

Satan, the great imitator of Divine methods, has established a kingdom which functions through delegated authority. We are admonished to wrestle against authorities in the heavenlies (see Ephesians 6:12). These wicked rulers have received delegated authority from Satan himself. Therefore, *the strong man* refers to either Satan himself, or to an authority which Satan has delegated. Just as in the United States Army certain officers and non-commissioned soldiers are put in charge of specific operations, in like manner, demons are assigned the responsibility of carrying out Satan's plans of attack. Demons, which act by the authority of their master, become the "strong men" against whom we must fight. Therefore, it is important for us to identify both the presence and objectives of such "strong men."

ENTER The House

Who is able to enter into the strong man's house? That

is, who is stronger than the strong man? The obvious answer is, "Jesus." Jesus is stronger than the devil. Who else is stronger than the strong man? Anyone to whom Jesus Christ has delegated His authority. All whom Jesus called and commissioned were given this authority. It was given to the twelve apostles (see Matthew 10:1); it was given to the seventy (see Luke 10: 1,19); it was given to every believer:

He said to them, 'Go into all the world and preach the good news to all creation...And these signs will accompany those who believe: In my name they will drive out demons...' (Mark 16:15,17)

The believer must know his authority; otherwise, he will never be able to enter into spiritual warfare with faith to overcome. Each Christian must learn that he has power over any and every demonic strong man. We, as true believers in the Lord Jesus Christ, can bind and cast out demons.

I have given you authority to trample on snakes and scorpions and to overcome all the power of the enemy; nothing will harm you. (Luke 10:19)

The Strong Man's HOUSE

The strong man's house is the person's body where he dwells and from which he rules:

When the unclean spirit is gone out of a man, he walketh through dry places, seeking rest, and findeth none. Then he saith, I will return into MY HOUSE from whence I came out... (Matthew 12:43,44)

Furthermore, the strong man's house is called his palace: *when a strong man armed keepeth his palace, his goods are in peace* (Luke 11:21 KJ).

A king lives in a palace. A palace is a seat of governmental authority. Thus, the strong man's house is his "palace"– the place from which he rules. His palace is often a person's body, but it can just as well be a household, church, community or nation.

When Jesus met the Gadarene demoniac, it was determined that this man was indwelt by a legion of spirits. A Roman legion comprised from five thousand to six thousand soldiers. When Jesus demanded, *What is your name?* the demonic strong man answered, *My name is Legion, for we are many* (Mark 5:9). Thus, one demon answered in behalf of many others. Legion was the ruler spirit, and the other indwelling spirits were under his authority. Legion's "palace" was this poor man's body, from which he directed the activities of a hoard of demons.

SPOIL His House

The Greek word for "spoil" occurs in two forms in Matthew 12:29 - *diarpazo* and *harapzo*. The force of these verbs denotes "an intensive spoiling, plundering and snatching away." In Luke 11:22 the word for spoil is *skulon*, which denotes "arms stripped from a foe." These words paint a dramatic picture of the effectiveness of the believer in binding the strong man. Satan is stripped of his weapons (see Luke 11:21,22), and all that he has previously captured is reclaimed.

Satan has plundered many things from Christians. In some cases he has taken away their joy, peace, purity, power, hope, faith and love. The fruits and gifts of the Holy Spirit are the rightful inheritances of the believer. The devil is out to steal these blessings, leaving God's children without power and Christian character. It is time that we get angry at the devil; angry enough to wage offensive warfare against him and regain all that he has plundered from our lives.

BIND the Strong Man

Binding is a tactic of spiritual warfare by which demonic powers are immobilized. When a demon is bound, he is prevented from carrying out his assignment. He is rendered helpless to proceed with his plots and plans.

The Greek word for bind is *deo*, which literally means "to tie or fasten." For example, an animal is bound to keep it from straying. *Go to the village ahead of you, and at once you will find a donkey TIED there...* (Matthew 21:2).

The word "bind" has special application to captives: *Now Herod had arrested John and BOUND HIM and put him in prison (Matthew 14:3). Then the king told the attendants, TIE HIM HAND AND FOOT, and throw him outside, into the darkness (Matthew 22:13). They BOUND HIM, led him away and handed him over to Pilate, the governor* (Matthew 27:2).

From the above passages we understand that the binding of a demonic strong man renders that spirit incapable of carrying out his assigned evil. He is restrained and immobilized. Binding is not an end in itself; it is a means to an end. The goal is to spoil the devil's house, and in order to accomplish this the strong man must first be bound.

FIRST Bind The Strong Man

The word "first" signifies priority. If one expects to spoil the devil's house, to regain all that the devil has stolen, then one MUST first bind the strong man. This is a hard and fast principle of spiritual warfare.

This principle of first binding the strong man applies to every level of spiritual warfare. Such binding is important to the deliverance of an individual from tormenting, defiling, oppressing and hindering spirits. Also, the strong man must first be bound when the believer wages warfare against ruler spirits over families, churches, cities and nations.

SCRIPTURAL EXAMPLES

To reiterate, we have learned from Matthew 12:29 that a vital principle of spiritual warfare is to "first bind the strong man." Since to "first bind the strong man" is a valid priority, we should expect to find examples of this principle throughout Bible history. Therefore, let us now examine several passages with this truth in mind.

Moses and Aaron Confront Pharaoh
Exodus 3-14

God raised up Moses and Aaron as a deliverance team. They were sent to deliver God's people from Egyptian oppression. What was their first move? They went to the elders of Israel and proclaimed liberty to the captives (see Exodus 3:16,17). The ministry of Jesus was the same - He fulfilled the prophecy of Isaiah to deliver us from bondage and oppression.

...the Lord has anointed me to preach good news to the poor. He has sent me to bind up the brokenhearted, to proclaim freedom for the captives and release from darkness for the prisoners. (Isaiah 61:1)

God's people, who were in Egyptian bondage, were told that God had heard their cries by reason of their affliction and that God was moving to deliver them.

Deliverance? For Christians? Yes! And still God's people must be told that God wants them to be set free. Many have not yet heard or believed that *on Mount Zion will be deliverance* (Obadiah 17); and that God has decreed. *Let the oppressed go free* (Isaiah 58:6 KJ). So, today the message of deliverance is being proclaimed the world over. Multitudes of God's people are oppressed of the devil, yet they do not know what to do about it. Therefore, God has raised up a corps of anointed ministers and sent them out to proclaim the good news of deliverance from evil spirits.

After Moses and Aaron had gone to the elders of Israel, they next went directly to Pharaoh and entered into a confrontation with the Egyptian ruler and his magicians. They did not incite the Israelites to civil disobedience. The Israelites were not told to make placards decrying the injustices done them and march before the pyramids. In other words, they did not war in the flesh, for the weapons of their warfare were not carnal but mighty in God to the pulling down of strongholds (see II Corinthians 10:3-5).

The contest between Moses and Aaron and the court of Pharaoh depicts spiritual warfare in slow motion. It was not warfare against the man Pharaoh but against principalities and powers in the heavenlies. The Satanic hierarchy utilizes men, but men are not the true enemies. WHEN THE POWERS IN THE HEAVENLIES ARE BOUND, THEN THE

MEN USED BY THE DEVIL WILL EITHER REPENT AND SUBMIT TO THE WAYS OF GOD OR ELSE THEY WILL BE REMOVED.

So, the warfare began and the tide of battle went back and forth. God's servants turned water into blood, and this miracle was duplicated by the magicians. When frogs were called forth throughout Egypt, the occultists did the same.

Note: The natural thing to expect would be that the occultists would have canceled the plagues brought on through Moses and Aaron, but instead they intensified the plagues which already existed. This is characteristic of the devil's work!

The ten plagues which God sent upon Egypt were blows against the gods of Egypt. The Egyptians worshipped the Nile River, frogs and cattle. Therefore, the plagues represented warfare *against the rulers, against the authorities, against the powers of this dark world and against the spiritual forces of evil in the heavenly realms* (Ephesians 6: 12).

Pharaoh and his crew remained obstinate. Pharaoh hardened his heart and refused to repent and obey God's command. So, eventually Pharaoh led his army in pursuit of the departing Israelites, and the Egyptian army was drowned in the Red Sea.

Through spiritual warfare, utilizing spiritual weapons, God's servants attacked the strong men of idolatry over Egypt. Satan had employed Pharaoh as his human agent. In the end, God's people were delivered from bondage and Pharaoh was destroyed. He had multiple opportunities to repent and obey God, but he refused.

Gideon and the Midianites
Judges 6-7

Again the Israelites did evil in the eyes of the Lord, and for seven years he gave them into the hands of the Midianites.
(Judges 6:1)

The Midianites came as destroyers in the land. They came like a plague of grasshoppers which destroyed the increase of the earth until nothing was left. The people cried unto Jehovah, and their merciful God called Gideon to deliver His people. Gideon felt completely unworthy for such a responsibility but finally submitted to God's will.

Gideon's first assignment was to destroy the altar to Baal which was in his father's house. Why? Because God's people had fallen into idolatry, and the curse upon them could not be lifted until the idol was removed.

The strong man over Israel was Baal, a demonic prince spirit who found human instrumentality in Gideon's own father. So, Gideon took his father's oxen and pulled down the altar of Baal.

The destruction of the idol caused an uproar in the city. (People get upset when their idols are attacked!) When they confronted Gideon's father, Joash, he defended his son's action and declared that if Baal needed protecting, then Baal ought to be able to fight for himself.

The spiritual warfare began. Gideon's strange weapons were trumpets, torches and pitchers. Such weapons would be considered puny in the eyes of men, but they were mighty in God to the pulling down of strongholds. Because the powers of Baal had been bound, Gideon's army gained a quick and complete victory. The two princes of Midian, Oreb and Zeeb, were slain and God's people had rest.

Elijah and the Prophets of Baal
I Kings 17-18

God sent Elijah to King Ahab to pronounce a judgment of drought upon the land. It did not rain for three and a half years. Then Elijah summoned all the people of Israel along with four hundred prophets of Baal to join him on Mt. Carmel for decision time. Who was the true God? and would Israel recognize and serve the true God?

The strong man over Israel was Baalism. The human instrumentality was King Ahab and wicked Queen Jezebel. The spiritual warfare began. Two altars were built and a sacrificial animal placed upon each one. One altar was unto Baal and the other unto Jehovah God. The God who answered by fire would be the true God.

The Baalites shrieked, jumped up and down and cut themselves with knives, but the god Baal was powerless to answer. Then Elijah quietly called upon the Lord and fire fell from heaven and consumed the water-soaked sacrifice. Whereupon the people fell on their faces and proclaimed, *The Lord - he is God! The Lord - he is God!* (1 Kings 18:39).

The four hundred prophets of Baal were executed in the Kishon Valley, and the rain came. Before God's judgment ended both Ahab and Jezebel were slain and, as prophesied, the dogs licked up their blood. Elijah had directly attacked the strong man, Baalism. Because God's people repented of their sin they were delivered. All those whom Satan had employed as his instruments were killed, including Ahab and Jezebel. The spirit of Jezebel is characterized by a stubborn refusal to repent. *I have given her (Jezebel) time to repent of her immorality, but she is unwilling* (Revelation 2:21).

When the strong man is bound, those through whom Satan is working have an opportunity to repent; if they refuse to repent, they are removed. Ahab and Jezebel were removed through death.

David And The Philistines
I Samuel 17-18

Here is the story of another strong man and his downfall. David was yet a young man, probably a teenager, when God called him to bring deliverance to the nation. David was a shepherd boy. What did he know about warfare? While tending the sheep he had learned the weapons of warfare. With his slingshot and his shepherd's rod, he had killed a lion and a bear, which had attacked his flock. Therefore, when the time came to face Goliath, the strong man of the Philistines, David had assurance that he would be victorious.

Today, God is training His army. The school of deliverance is found in the sheepfold known as the local church. The "sheep" in the body of Christ are the beneficiaries of deliverance, as pastors become familiar with the weapons that are not carnal but which are mighty in God to the pulling down of Satan's strongholds.

Goliath had intimidated God's entire army. In all Israel there was no faith in God for victory. The giant towered above God's soldiers and put fear into their hearts. But there was one who was not afraid. David knew that God was with him. His weapons had already been tested and proven effective.

When Goliath was slain, the whole army of Israel suddenly become brave and aggressive. They chased the fleeing Philistines and *spoiled their tents* (I Samuel 17:53

KJ). Indeed, one must first bind the strong man and then spoil his house. The strong man over Israel was the principality of "Intimidation."

Our deliverance team ministered in a church which had once been ruled over by a strong man of intimidation. The pastor of that church told us the story. One day he was alone praying in the altar area of the church's auditorium. He heard footsteps walking in the back of the room. He continued to pray and did not look up. The steps continued. He could hear the legs of the one who was walking as they brushed up against the seats. The footsteps were going back and forth between the pews. Finally, his curiosity got the upper hand, and he looked up to see who was there. He saw a giant of a person who had the head of a pig with large tusks. He knew that this being was demonic.

The pastor said, "I was very afraid, but I told the evil thing that it must leave." The creature said, "No, I will not leave. I rule over the last two rows of pews of this church. I am the spirit of Intimidation."

This was a denominational church, and the pastor was seeking to lead the church into truths of God that were foreign to most of the members. Those who opposed the pastor would sit on the last two rows each Sunday with their arms folded, attempting to intimidate the pastor as he preached. The pastor continued to command the Spirit of Intimidation to leave. After several minutes of spiritual warfare, the evil presence reluctantly turned and walked out.

A Satanic strong man of Intimidation was working through Goliath. David approached the giant in faith:

David said to the Philistine, 'You come against me with sword and spear and javelin, but I come against you in the name of the Lord Almighty, the God of the armies of Israel, whom you have defied. This day the Lord will hand you

*over to me, and I'll strike you down and cut off your head.
Today I will give the carcasses of the Philistine army to the
birds of the air and the beasts of the earth, and the whole
world will know that there is a God in Israel. All those
gathered here will know that it is not by sword or spear
that the Lord saves, for the battle is the Lord's, and he will
give all of you into our hands.* (I Samuel 17:45-47)

Let every true soldier in God's army go forth as David
did with the same boldness of faith and assault the
principalities and powers over nation, state, city, church and
family.

The Church and Its Persecutors
Acts 12

*It was about this time that King Herod arrested some who
belonged to the church, intending to persecute them. He
had James, the brother of John, put to death with the
sword. When he saw that this pleased the Jews, he
proceeded to seize Peter also.* (Acts 12:1-3)

Who was the church's enemy? The enemy was the
devil. King Herod was an instrument in the hands of Satan.
The church went to prayer. Prayer is a companion to and a
vital part of spiritual warfare. Prayer causes God to activate
His army of angels in our behalf. Remember that when
Moses interceded for Israel following their sin with the
golden calf, the Lord responded by saying, *I will send an
angel before thee and drive out the Canaanites, Amorites,
Hittites, Perizzites, Hivites and Jebusite* (Exodus 33:2).

Jehovah God is the "Lord of Hosts." "Hosts" means
armies. God has more than one army. He has an army in
heaven made up of mighty angels with Michael the

archangel in charge. God also has an army on earth - the Church of the Living God. The Church, the Bride of Christ, is described as *majestic as troups with banners* (Solomon's Song 6:4).

Prayer and spiritual warfare go hand in hand. This is seen again in Ephesians 6:14-17 where we find a description of the Christian's armor. Six pieces of armor are identified: the belt of truth, the breastplate of righteousness, feet fitted with the readiness that comes from the gospel of peace, the shield of faith, the helmet of salvation and the sword of the Spirit which is the word of God. THEN we read,

> *And PRAY in the Spirit on all occasions with all kinds of prayers and requests. With this in mind, be alert and always keep on praying for all the saints.*
> (Ephesians 6:18)

The persecuted church at Jerusalem began to bombard the heavenlies. While Peter was in prison, prayer was made for him without ceasing (see Acts 12:5). How did God answer their prayers? He sent an angel to deliver Peter out of prison!

Nevertheless, Peter's supernatural rescue did not lead King Herod to repentance. Instead, Herod had the guards executed. Then Herod stood and delivered a public address to the people, whereupon the people shouted, *This is the voice of god, not of a man* (Acts 12:22). Upon hearing the response of the people, Herod's heart was filled with pride, and because he failed to give God the glory, the Lord smote him, and he was eaten of worms and died (see Acts 12:21-23).

The strong man over the church at Jerusalem was "Persecution." When the church prayed, the strong man

34

was bound, and his house was spoiled. This principality over the church had brought about the death of John and was holding Peter captive, but Peter was delivered by the ministry of an angel sent by God in response to the church's intercession. Herod, the human instrument used by Satan to persecute the church, did not repent; therefore, he died. *But the word of God continued to increase and spread* (Acts 12:24).

Daniel and The Captivity
Daniel 9-10

This is an important passage which will be examined more closely in a subsequent chapter. Nonetheless, let it here be noted that the principle of first confronting the strong man is again exemplified.

Daniel and his people had been captives of war for seventy years, the length of the judgment which God had pronounced upon them because of their sins. When Daniel prayed, God sent forth angels to bind the "Prince of Persia," the ruler spirit over Persia. This demonic prince controlled the affairs of Persia, and the Jews could not be freed from captivity until the strong man over Persia had been bound.

Michael and another angel continued the warfare in the heavenlies until the spiritual prince and kings of Persia were immobilized (see Daniel 10: 13,20). Just as soon as their goal was accomplished, the Spirit of God moved upon King Cyrus who made the following proclamation:

The Lord, the God of heaven, has given me all the kingdoms of the earth and he has appointed me to build a temple for him at Jerusalem in Judah. Anyone of his people among you - may his God be with him, and let him go up to Jerusalem in Judah and build the temple of the

Lord, the God of Israel, the God who is in Jerusalem. And
the people of any place where survivors may be living are
to provide him with silver and gold, with goods and
livestock, and with freewill offerings for the temple of God
in Jerusalem.   (Ezra 1:2-41)

What an amazing turn of events! King Cyrus suddenly reversed a seventy year policy, and the Jews were free to return to Jerusalem with financial support for the restoration of their temple. Even before Cyrus was born, it had been prophesied by Isaiah that he would do this very thing (see Isaiah 44:24.28).

When the Prince of Persia was bound by God's warring angels, King Cyrus was free to obey God. He chose to be God's instrument for the restoration of the Jews. Since Cyrus obeyed God, he was not removed from kingship.

May God open the eyes of our understanding that we may discern the operation of the Satanic powers in the heavenlies. Principalities and powers in the air are the real rulers of this dark world. They employ human agents, but the evil in the world is orchestrated by them. Everyone who longs to see the overthrow of wickedness and the enthronement of righteousness will zealously take up his weapons of spiritual warfare and bind the powers of the devil coming against himself, his family, his community and his nation.

IV

The Keys of the Kingdom

Matthew 16:13-19

We have already established that the authority of the believer is the authority of Jesus Himself. This authority is borne in His name. Those who bear His name are those who are related to Him through the new birth. These have become the sons of God and heirs of God's promises. The commission which Christ gave to His Church cannot be carried out by human resources. Only in the authority of the Name greater than Satan's can a demon be expelled. For this reason Jesus said to the newly commissioned Church. *And these signs will accompany those who believe: In my name they will drive out demons...* (Mark 16:17) (emphasis mine).

Before the first believers could move in His authority, it was essential for them to know who He was. Therefore, Jesus began to ask His followers questions designed to discover their understanding of His true identity.

> *When Jesus came to the region of Caesarea Philippi, he asked his disciples. 'Who do people say the Son of man is?' They replied, 'Some say John the Baptist; others say Elijah: and still others, Jeremiah or one of the prophets.' 'But what about you?' he asked, 'Who do you say I am?' Simon Peter answered, 'You are the Christ, the Son of the living God.'* (Matthew 16:13-16)

You can be sure that Peter's answer, given on behalf of

the twelve, blessed the heart of Jesus. They each believed that He was the Messiah, God's Son. Now He could reveal to them the great truth of imparted authority. He could tell them of His Church and prophesy to them of His Church's coming victory over Satan. He could share with them the secret of spiritual authority through the keys of the kingdom.

> *Jesus replied, 'Blessed are you. Simon son of Jonah, for this was not revealed to you by man, but by my Father in heaven. And I tell you that you are Peter, and on this rock I will build my church, and the gates of Hades will not overcome it.* (Matthew 16:17-18)

The name *Peter* means *stone*. The little stone had correctly identified the Big Rock! Peter had received a divine revelation. Jesus disclosed to Peter that His Church would be a militant Church, assaulting the very gates of Hades.

The expression "gates of Hades" is apparently taken from the Old Testament references to the gates of a city as being the place of city government. A king would meet with his elders in the gates of the city to conduct courts and also devise plans for war. "Hades" is the correct translation rather than "hell" as rendered in the King James edition. Hades is equated with death and the region of departed spirits. Satan is not in hell, nor is he the ruler over hell. Eventually he will be the principle prisoner in that terrible place. The Lake of Fire is a place *prepared for the devil and his angels* (Matthew 25:41).

By His reference to "the gates of Hades," Jesus is declaring that Satan will never be able to destroy His Church and bring it down to death. Neither will the power of Satan be able to withstand the assault of His Church's offensive against him. All of Satan's strategy will be defeated, even in his "gates," before he can get his plans into operation. Christ's prophecy has yet to be fulfilled. His Church must rise up in her fullness of power and defeat the gates of Hades. We could well be the generation to witness this fulfillment.

Keys Of Authority

Verse 19 continues the teaching concerning Christ's Church and her authority. There is no break in the context. Jesus now tells the Church how she will conquer the gates of Hades.

> *I will give you the keys of the kingdom of heaven; and whatever you bind on earth will be bound in heaven, and whatever you loose on earth will be loosed in heaven.*
> (Matthew 16:19)

In order to defeat Satan in his gates. Jesus gives His church *the keys of the Kingdom of heaven.* Keys represent authority. These keys equip the Church with authority to bind and loose. To illustrate: when someone has keys to an automobile, he can use those keys to unlock the automobile, start the engine and drive it away. He has loosed the automobile. Then, he can stop the car and use the key to turn off the engine and lock the doors. He has bound the automobile. This pictures for us the power to loose or bind through the use of appropriate keys.

The Lord has given "keys" (plural) to the Church. He identifies the keys for us and says they are the keys "of the kingdom of heaven." That is, they are keys of spiritual authority. Notice that the keys are not "to" the Kingdom but are "of" the Kingdom. The keys are not for entrance into the kingdom, as some have supposed, but represent the very authority of heaven itself. The Church is invested with the authority of the One who sits on the throne of heaven. She has the authority of Christ. With one key she can bind, and with the other key she can loose.

We must learn to use these two keys, for they are the keys of authority enabling us to bind Satan and loose his captives. What needs to be bound? Are there satanic activities in your life, your family, your church, your community or your nation which need to be stopped? The key of authority to bind is given for this purpose. The church holds the key.

What needs to be loosed? Are there persons in bondage to sickness, poverty, addictions, fears and hurts? The power to loose is demonstrated by Jesus when He met a woman who was bound by a spirit of infirmity. When Jesus was criticized for healing the woman on the Sabbath, He replied:

> *You hypocrites! Doesn't each of you on the Sabbath untie his ox or donkey from the stall and lead it out to give it water? Then should not this woman, a daughter of Abraham, whom Satan has kept bound for eighteen long years, be set free on the Sabbath day from what bound her?* (Luke 13:15-16)

Through the power of healing, Jesus loosed a woman from the bondage of Satan. Healing and deliverance are loosing ministries. The Church holds the key, for Jesus said to His Church, *I will give you the keys of the kingdom of heaven.*

The Greek word for "loose" is *luo*. It simply means to unbind or release. Jesus illustrated the loosing of the bound woman by comparing it to the loosing of a tethered animal. A tethered animal is restrained; it is bound; it is not free.

When the rope that binds the animal is loosed, then the animal is free to be led by his master to refreshing water. Thus, Jesus illustrated how Satan binds persons, even God's own children, and hinders them from reaching the blessings of God. Those in bondage need loosing by others who have the compassion and authority of Jesus.

There is yet another facet of this truth to explore. Jesus taught that the binding and loosing of things on earth were in direct relationship to their being bound or loosed in heaven.

Whatever you bind on earth will be bound in heaven, and whatever you loose on earth will be loosed in heaven.
(Matthew 16:19)

To understand the exactness of what Jesus taught, we must examine the Greek grammar in the verse. The verbs translated "will be bound" and "will be loosed" are perfect, passive participles. This means that whatever is bound or loosed on earth are the things which are presently in a state of having been forbidden or permitted in the heavenlies. The binding and loosing in the heavens does not refer to something God does for us, but to our doing what God has given us authority to do. The meaning of the verse can be rendered thus: "Whatever is bound or loosed on earth is that which is already in a state of having been bound or loosed in the heavenlies." (See the footnote to Matthew 16:19 in the *Amplified Bible*.)

Matthew 16 gives us an understanding of how the believer's authority is employed. In order to change anything Satan is doing on earth, the believer must first take authority over the strongman in the heavenlies who controls the situation on earth. The believer changes conditions on earth by first binding the principalities and powers of *the ruler of the kingdom of the air* (Ephesians 2:2), and by loosing Satan's captives from the power of his highest echelons of wickedness in the heavenlies. The Church has the "keys" for defeating Satan, but the keys are of no value unless they are used. Merely to boast that we have the keys accomplishes nothing.

Attacks From Within

A second reference to binding and loosing appears in Matthew 18. Jesus here repeats what He has said in Chapter 16; however, it is couched in a different context. In the account already reviewed, Jesus was speaking of attacks of Satan coming from outside the Church. As we have seen, the Church has authority to deal with such assaults.

Now, the Lord tells the Church that it also has authority to deal with Satan's attacks from within the Church when Satan works through one or more of its members. Jesus uses the example of two persons who have fallen out of fellowship, and the offending party refuses to repent and be reconciled. In such ways Satan introduces spiritual cancers into the body of Christ. What is to be done?

If your brother sins against you, go and show him his fault, just between the two of you. If he listens to you, you have won your brother over. But if he will not listen, take one or two others along, so that every matter may be established by the testimony of two or three witnesses. If he refuses to listen to them, tell it to the church; and if he refuses to listen even to the church, treat him as you would a pagan or a tax collector. I tell you the truth, whatever you bind on earth will be bound in heaven, and whatever you loose on earth will be loosed in heaven.

(Matthew 18:15-18)

Internal conflict within the Church issues from the working of Satan, and the basic battle is not against flesh and blood, but against the powers of Satan enthroned in the heavenlies. If the conflict cannot be resolved between the two persons, then witnesses to the grievance are called upon to judge and resolve the problem. If the person found to be at fault refuses to heed the witnesses, the issue is brought before the governing authorities of the Church. If the person judged to be in the wrong refuses to heed the counsel of the Church, and elects to remain a problem within the fellowship, then there is one further recourse. It is a very serious recourse and should not be employed until all of the previous attempts at reconciliation have been thoroughly pursued.

When a member of the fellowship is stubborn and refuses discipline, he cannot be left to disturb the body at will. He is to be treated as *a pagan or a tax collector*. That is, he is dealt with as one who is outside the spiritual covering of the Church. The Church has no spiritual authority over the lost, but it does have authority over its members (see I Corinthians 5:12). When a person refuses discipline and correction, he then forfeits his rights as a member of the body. When the protective covering of the Church is lifted, he is made vulnerable to Satan and becomes his prey. The Church has loosed Satan upon the unruly person. Genuine excommunication is indeed a very serious matter.

The Apostle Paul led the Church at Corinth into carrying out this sort of discipline. There was an unrepentant man in the fellowship who was continuing to live in an incestuous relationship. Paul sent the church these instructions:

43

When you are assembled in the name of our Lord Jesus and I am with you in spirit, and the power of our Lord Jesus is present, hand this man over to Satan, so that the sinful nature may be destroyed and his spirit saved on the day of our Lord. (I Corinthians 5:4-5)

This discipline was no freelance procedure by Paul. It was done in conjunction with full Church authority and by carefully following the necessary spiritual procedures. The turning over of a person to Satan was done:

(1) **In the name of our Lord Jesus**. The Church could not execute this judgment except by divine power. When Paul told them to carry it out in the name of the Lord Jesus, he was affirming that they indeed had the authority to act. When and how did the Church obtain such authority? This authority was given to the Church by Jesus as found in Matthew 16:18.

(2) **In the unity of the Spirit**. Paul said, *I am with you in spirit* (I Corinthians 5:3-4). This same unity of agreement is reflected in Matthew 18:19-20. Immediately following the declaration of power to bind and loose the power of Satan into a situation, Jesus said: *Again. I tell you that if two of you on earth AGREE about anything you ask for, it will be done for you by my Father in heaven. For where two or three COME TOGETHER in my name, there am I with them.* Unity in the Spirit is necessary for the Church to execute her spiritual authority.

(3) **By a function of Church government**, carried out in the presence of the assembly. *When you are assembled in the name of our Lord Jesus...* (v. 4) correlates with Matthew 18:17, *Tell it to the church.*

(4) With sorrow of heart over the man's condition, but with the positive goal *that the sinful nature may be destroyed and his spirit saved on the day of the Lord* (v. 5).

The only way back into the fellowship for this sinner would be through the door of repentance. In his second letter to the church at Corinth we discover that the man had repented, and the church was instructed to forgive him and restore him (see: II Corinthians 2:6-11).

Next, observe how Paul's exhortation to the Corinthians to forgive the repentant sinner parallels the teaching of Jesus on forgiveness in Matthew 18:21-35. Jesus said that an unforgiving person would be *turned over to the jailors to be tortured*, until he should pay his debt of forgiveness of another. If the Church has loosed Satan upon one of its members as a means of discipline, and those who took such action fail to forgive that person when he repents, then they are subject to the same torment from demons which the disciplined man has received (See Matthew 18:32-34). Because of this possibility Paul wrote to Corinth:

> *If anyone has caused grief, he has not so much grieved me as he has grieved all of you, to some extent--not to put it too severely. The punishment inflicted on him by the majority is sufficient for him. Now instead, you ought to forgive and comfort him, so that he will not be overwhelmed by excessive sorrow. I urge you, therefore, to reaffirm your love for him. The reason I wrote you was to see if you would stand the test and be obedient in everything. If you forgive anyone, I also forgive him. And what I have forgiven--if there was anything to forgive--I* **have forgiven in the sight of Christ for your sake, in order that Satan might not outwit us. For we are not unaware of his schemes.**
>
> (II Corinthians 2:5-11. Emphasis mine.)

The Church is the instrument of the Kingdom of God. Through the instrumentality of the Church, the Kingdom of God is brought upon the earth even as it is in heaven. Therefore, the Church must be aggressive in spiritual warfare, binding and loosing with the keys of authority given her. The Church must be vigilant to overthrow every assault from without and also those that come from within. Satan is the instigator of all such assaults. The devil can do no more than the believer and the Church permit him to do.

V

Warfare in the Heavenlies

Now that we have seen from Matthew 12 that the strong man must be bound, and from Matthew 16 and 18 that the Church has the keys to bind and loose, let us see an illustration of warfare in the heavenlies from the book of Daniel.

As we turn to Daniel, we find that there was something that needed to be changed on earth. God's people were in bondage in a foreign land. They longed for freedom to return to their land. How would this freedom be accomplished?

According to the principle which we have learned in the New Testament, the way to change things on earth is to bind and loose in the heavenlies. Let us observe this principle enacted in Daniel's day.

In the ninth chapter of Daniel we find Daniel making an exciting discovery through reading the prophecies of Jeremiah.

In the first year of his (Darius') reign I, Daniel, under-stood from the Scriptures, according to the word of the Lord given to Jeremiah the prophet, that the desolation of Jerusalem would last seventy years.   (Daniel 9:2)

Daniel had been taken a prisoner of war by the Babylonians when he was but a youth. He and many of his people had been in captivity for over sixty years. Daniel had grown up to be a mighty prophet of God. Now, he finds that Jeremiah had prophesied that the Jews would be freed from their exile at the end of seventy years. He realized that the seventy years were almost expired, and his heart was turned to seek the Lord with spiritual intensity.

We should note that God has a timing in all that He does. Daniel was living in a momentous day of God's moving among His people. We, too, are living in a time of special visitation from God. We are seeing the fulfillment of Joel's prophecy that God will pour out His Spirit upon all flesh (see Joel 2:28-29). This prophecy began to be fulfilled on the day of Pentecost and now the climax of its fulfillment has burst upon us. The past two decades of the Church have been significant years as the Pentecostal power is being restored and the gospel preached amid signs and wonders.

A part of the spiritual restoration of our day involves deliverance from demons and spiritual warfare in the heavenlies. This ministry began its restoration only a few short years ago. It began as a tiny trickle, met with great resistance by tradition-bound Christianity; but the thrust of spiritual warfare has now become a mighty, rushing river of cleansing power within the body of Christ.

The same message that God spoke to Pharaoh through Moses and Aaron is again resounded in our day: *"Let my people go, so that they may worship me."* (Exodus 8:1). God's people are in many bondages today. They are in bondages to fear, depression, lust, addictions, anger, worry, religious traditions, complacency, sickness and many other things. These bondages are demonic. God's people are not free to serve God as they should. But God has heard their cries just as He heard the cries of the Israelites suffering under Egyptian oppression, and He has said. *"Let my people go."* God is saying the same thing to the powers of Satan holding the Church in bondage today. When Daniel under-

48

stood that it was God's timing to deliver His people. Daniel activated himself spiritually.

> *So I turned to the Lord God and pleaded with him in prayer and petition, in fasting, and in sackcloth and ashes. I prayed to the Lord my God and confessed: 'O Lord, the great and awesome God, who keeps his covenant of love with all who love him and obey his commands, we have sinned and done wrong. We have been wicked and have rebelled; we have turned away from your commands and laws. We have not listened to your servants the prophets, who spoke in your name to our kings, our princes and our fathers, and to all the people of the land.'* (Daniel 9:3-6)

Our response to God must be the same as that of Daniel. God is moving in our day. He is preparing His bride for His return. He is about to establish His kingdom on earth even as it is in heaven. It is time for God's people to seek the Lord with all their hearts—with prayer and fasting. It is time for confession of sins: personal sins and the sins of our nation. It is time for full repentance, a turning from every sin and a turning to God in a commitment of faithfulness and holiness.

When we come to the tenth chapter of Daniel, we discover that a few more years have transpired. The seventy years of captivity prophesied by Jeremiah are fulfilled. It is time for the captives to be set free. Daniel is bombarding heaven with prayer and fasting. He is seeking understanding of the prophecy of Jeremiah and of visions from the Lord. He has fasted and prayed for three weeks.

> *At that time I, Daniel, mourned for three weeks. I ate no choice food; no meat or wine touched my lips; and I used no lotions at all until the three weeks were over.*
> (Daniel 10:2-3)

It must have seemed to Daniel that his prayers were not heard. Twenty days had gone by and there was no word from God. There are times in each of our lives when we pray, and it seems that the heavens have turned to brass. Time is running out, and there is no answer from heaven. But we can know that when we pray in faith, our prayers are heard. We may not see the answer to our prayers; but the answer is on the way, and our prayers have set things into motion in the heavenlies.

On the twenty-first day of Daniel's fast there appeared unto him an angel with this message:

> *Do not be afraid, Daniel. Since the first day that you set your mind to gain understanding and to humble yourself before your God, your words were heard, and I have come in response to them.* (Daniel 10:12)

Where had this angel been for three weeks? Are not angels able to travel at the speed of light? The angel admitted that Daniel's prayer was heard in heaven the very first day that it was offered. Why had it taken the angel so long to get there with the answer?

As the angel continued to talk, he cleared up all of Daniel's questions:

> *But the prince of the Persian kingdom resisted me twenty one days. Then Michael, one of the chief princes, came to help me, because I was detained there with the king of Persia.* (Daniel 10:13)

The angel dispatched from God had been engaged in warfare for three weeks. Why? Because this was the means by which Daniel's prayers for the release of his people would be accomplished. Before the Jews could be released

50

from captivity, the ruler spirit over Persia must be bound. (Note: the Persians had conquered the Babylonians after the Jews were first taken into captivity, so they were now under Persian control.)

The *prince of the Persian kingdom* was no earthly ruler, but the prince was a demonic power assigned over that nation by Satan. Before the Jewish captives in Persia could be released on earth, the powers of the demonic kingdom over Persia must first be bound in the heavenlies. These powers worked through the earthly ruler, King Cyrus. Cyrus would not release the Jews until the demonic power which controlled him was bound. The angel was fulfilling his assignment by wrestling the demonic powers over Persia.

We know that the angel was successful in binding the Persian strong man because we read of the results. Soon after this warfare in the heavenlies. King Cyrus woke up one morning with a new thought in his mind. Why not let the Jews return to their own country? In fact, he decided to help them return. Why had Cyrus had such a change of attitude? Because the powers which controlled him had been bound.

The angel from heaven was not being prevented from bringing the message to Daniel, but he was occupied with answering Daniel's prayer. After three weeks he took time out to bring the message to Daniel, and then returned to fight with *the prince of the Persian kingdom* until that prince was bound. He asked Daniel this question: "*Do you know why I have come to you?*" (Daniel 10:20). Daniel, do you really understand what is going on? Do you comprehend that your prayers are being answered through warfare in the heavenlies?

Soon I will return to fight against the prince of Persia, and when I go, the prince of Greece will come.
(Daniel 10:20b)

When God's angelic messengers had completed their assignment of binding the strong man over Persia, the Jews were released to return to Jerusalem. This left a spiritual vacuum over Persia which would soon be filled. Thus, the angel explained to Daniel that after the release of the Jews from captivity a new ruler spirit would take control over Persia. This new Ruler would be "the prince of Greece." In other words, the ruler spirit over Greece would extend his dominion to include Persia. We know that this rule actually took place, because we can read about it in secular history books. At this time in history, there arose in Greece a military genius named Alexander the Great. He marshalled his armies and moved to the east, and he conquered the Medo-Persian Empire.

Everything we see taking place in history is a reflection of what is going on in the heavenlies. In this case, as Alexander the Great moved with his army on earth, the ruler spirit over Greece which worked through Alexander was moving parallel to him in the heavenlies, extending his dominion over another country. Things on earth were being bound and loosed as things in the heavenlies were bound and loosed.

Next the angel declared to Daniel, *But I will show thee that which is noted in the scripture of truth* (Daniel 10:21, KJV). Daniel will see the fulfillment of that which was spoken by Jeremiah. The Jews will return to Jerusalem.

Finally, the angel identified Michael as "your prince." There are not only demonic princes assigned over nations, but also God's holy messengers. When we go into spiritual warfare, we are not alone; the angels are there to fight along with us. If we could see into the heavenlies, as in an open vision, we would see what Elisha and his servant saw when they were surrounded by the Syrian army. The servant was afraid when he saw the Syrians surrounding the city.

> *"Don't be afraid," the prophet answered. "Those who are with us are more than those who are with them"...Then the Lord opened the servant's eyes, and he looked and saw the hills full of horses and chariots of fire all around Elisha.*
> (II Kings 6:16-17)

Jehovah God is called *The Lord of Hosts,* and "hosts" means armies. God has a heavenly army comprised of His mighty angels, and He has an army on earth called the Church. These two armies are merged when the saints are at war.

The question is sure to arise: Why not do what Daniel did? Why not simply pray and let the angels take care of the principalities and powers in the heavenlies? The Church has something that Daniel did not have. The Church has been given the keys of the Kingdom of Heaven. These keys were not given to men until Jesus conferred them upon His disciples in Matthew 16. The Church has the power to bind and loose in the heavenlies. This is why Paul prayed that the eyes of the Church's understanding would be enlightened in order that she might know *His incomparably great power for us who believe* (Ephesians 1:19).

The saints of God are rising. They represent only a remnant of the believers, but God has always worked through remnants. Nevertheless, the army of God is marching into battle. The ranks are increasing daily with those who recognize their authority in Christ over the principalities and powers of Satan and who are binding the ruler spirits over families, churches, cities and nations.

Satan's kingdom is being torn down, and the Kingdom of God is being established.

Arise, O saints, and *The God of peace will soon crush Satan under your feet* (Romans 16:20).

In A Vision

Spiritual warfare deals with spiritual entities in an unseen realm. Since we are not wrestling *against flesh and blood,* (Ephesians 6:12), our warfare is carried out by faith. Eventually, as we persist in spiritual wrestling in the heavenlies, we will see the evidence of our warfare as things on earth are bound and loosed.

In a vision from God, the author's associate in ministry, Jay Lee, was shown what happens when we bind the Devil and his demon spirits. The following is the account of the vision.

The Power of Binding and Loosing
by: Jay Lee

In a dramatic open vision God revealed to me the dynamic power He has given to His church–the power to bind the enemy, and the power to loose those whom the enemy has bound.

In the vision, the Lord transported me to Satan's headquarters, the unholy of unholies of the kingdom of darkness. In Satan's headquarters I saw an oblong, black table in the center of the room. There was a glowing, blue ball in the center of the table. (The Spirit later revealed to me that this ball represented the earth). Around the room. next to the walls, appeared dingy yellow flames of fire eight feet tall. (The Lord revealed to me that these flames were

54

demon spirits). In the center of the room, at the far end of the table, was another flame. This flame was the same dingy yellow color, but it was only half as tall as the other flames. Another marked difference in this flame was that it had what appeared to be sparklers flashing inside it. (The Lord revealed to me that this flame with the sparklers was Satan, and that the sparklers were a counterfeit of the radiant glory of God).

As I looked around the room, I became aware of a presence behind me in the room. When I turned to see what was behind me, I saw fourteen brilliant white columns of fire that were much larger and brighter and far more intimidating than the other flames in the room. (The Lord revealed to me that these columns of fire were an angelic host assigned by God to accompany me continually). This angelic escort was standing in a "V" formation, like a flock of geese in flight, and I was standing at the point of the "V".

When I discovered that I was protected from the back, I turned around to face Satan and his demonic host, and I immediately entered into spiritual warfare against them. Stretching out my hand, I pointed at the enemy and said in a loud voice, "IN THE NAME OF JESUS, I BIND YOU!" As soon as I had given this command, golden chains shot out from my outstretched hand and wrapped themselves tightly around each of the demonic spirits in the room, and also around Satan himself.

At this point Satan began to communicate with me in a very cautious way, fearing that I might enter into spiritual warfare again. He said, "Do you want to feed the hungry? Do you want to heal the sick? Do you want to have global outreach in your ministry? Fine, fine. We'll play along; only DON'T DO THAT THING." (The Lord revealed to me that the "thing" Satan was talking about was spiritual warfare.)

As I was pondering the things that Satan had said, and wondering why he was so fearful of the ministry of spiritual warfare, the Lord expanded the vision to reveal to me the answer.

A radiant light appeared high overhead, and the walls around the room started to open slowly. When the walls had opened, I was transported out of the chamber room and found myself flying over an immense field that stretched out in all directions. As I was moving through the air, I looked down and saw rows and rows of small piles of chains. (The Lord revealed to me that under these piles of chains were demon spirits that had once been very productive for the kingdom of darkness, but now they had been bound and rendered totally ineffective by Christians engaged in spiritual warfare). As I neared the edge of this vast field, the vision took on an entirely different perspective. It was as though I was looking through a window back into the natural world. There I saw demon spirits casting chains upon people who were walking about. These people were bound very securely by the chains which the demons cast. However, there were other people nearby who were, at the same time, taking authority over the demons and commanding the chains to be loosed. Whereupon, the chains which were wrapped around the people fell away like melted butter.

Next, I was transported back into the room where I first entered the vision. There was now a brighter light in the room, and I could see in greater detail the things that were in this room. I could see why Satan appeared so much shorter than the evil spirits stationed around the room. He was weighted down by a great pile of chains. I noticed that more and more bright golden chains continued to be applied to Satan. Yet, at the same time I saw some of the chains which were binding Satan begin to corrode and fall away. Also, at Satan's side I saw three small cartoon-like beings who were working desperately to remove the chains that bound Satan. These little creatures were sawing and pulling at the chains, but their efforts were futile.

I further noticed that the demon spirits standing around the sides of the room had very few chains on them. Some of these demons were only bound by the chains which I had cast upon them at the beginning of the vision. I asked the Lord the meaning of these new things of which I had become aware. He revealed to me that the new chains being applied were the results of Christians continually binding Satan. The reason some of the chains were falling off of Satan was because the Christians who had bound him, had lost faith in their authority to bind and loose. The Lord then showed me that the cartoon-like characters by the side of Satan represented the futility of the Kingdom of darkness to loose what God's servants have bound. Let every believer be persuaded that no power in Hell can loose that which is bound in the name of Jesus!

Then, the Lord showed me why the demon spirits around the room had few chains on them. These were spirits of deception which Christians had not yet discerned and, therefore, had not bound. These spirits were left free to continue their work of deception without confrontation from the ranks of the believers.

At this point the vision ended, and I was left with a powerful message for the body of Christ. Brothers and sisters in Christ, I exhort you to be aggressive in spiritual warfare daily, and I assure you that all binding and loosing that is done in faith has a tremendous impact upon the kingdom of darkness.

VI

Thy Kingdom Come

Let us quickly review a principle which we have discovered: BEFORE THE KINGDOM OF GOD IS ESTABLISHED ON EARTH, THE KINGDOM OF SATAN MUST BE OVERTHROWN.

Satan holds everything and everyone in the earth in his power until they are rescued. There was a time when each born-again believer was held in Satan's power. Before he was quickened he was dead in trespasses and sins, following the ways of the world and of the ruler of the kingdom of the air. (See Ephesians 2:1-2.) The new birth experience represents the power of Satan's kingdom being broken and the Kingdom of God being established in the heart of the new believer. *For he has rescued us from the dominion of darkness and brought us into the kingdom of the Son he loves* (Colossians 1:13). This principle holds true on whatever level it is applied, from an individual to a nation. God's Kingdom is never established until Satan's kingdom is overthrown.

In what we call "The Lord's Prayer," Jesus taught us to pray to the Heavenly Father. *Your kingdom come, your will be done on earth as it is in heaven* (Matthew 6:10). Wherever Jesus is Lord, the Kingdom of God has come to that place. When Jesus is Lord in your life, the Kingdom of God has come to you. When Jesus is Lord over your family, the church you attend, or the city where you live, then the Kingdom of God has come. When the Kingdom of God comes on earth, Jesus will be Lord over all.

In the twentieth chapter of Revelation we find a prophecy telling us that at the end of the age the Kingdom of God shall come fully upon the earth. This scripture confirms to us once again that the Kingdom of God cannot come until the rule of Satan is overthrown.

> *And I saw an angel coming down out of heaven. having the key to the Abyss and holding in his hand a great chain.*
> (Revelation 20:1)

Once again we find the "key" of authority. What is the angel going to do with the key and the great chain?

> *He seized the dragon, that ancient serpent, who is the devil, or Satan, and bound him a thousand years. He threw him into the Abyss, and locked and sealed it over him, to keep him from deceiving the nations anymore until the thousand years were ended. After that he must be set free for a short time.* (Revelation 20:2-3)

The strong man is bound. When he is bound, he is unable to deceive the nations any longer. Satan, who has caused so much chaos on earth for so long, is now chained and thrown into the Abyss for a thousand years. The next verse describes the ushering in of the millennial reign of Christ, when there will be a thousand years of perfect peace.

> *I saw thrones on which were seated those who had been given authority to judge. And I saw the souls of those who had been beheaded because of their testimony for Jesus and because of the word of God...They came to life and reigned with Christ a thousand years.*
> (Revelation 20:4)

THE KINGDOM OF GOD COMES ON EARTH
AS A RESULT OF SATAN'S BEING BOUND.

When the thousand years are over, Satan will be released
from his prison and will go out to deceive the nations in
the four corners of the earth–Gog and Magog–to gather
them for battle.   (Revelation 20:7-8)

When Satan is loose, the earth is in trouble. When-ever
Satan is bound, the Kingdom of God can come forth. As
soon as Satan is loosed, he immediately begins to deceive
the nations again, and war comes upon the earth. Then
comes the final doom of Satan together with all the fallen
angels.

And the devil, who deceived them, was thrown into the lake
of burning sulfur, where the beast and the false prophet
had been thrown. They will be tormented day and night
for ever and ever.   (Revelation 20:10)

Revelation 20 does not indicate that the saints will
participate in the final binding of Satan which ushers in the
millennial reign of Christ, but in Revelation 12 the Scripture
teaches that the saints will defeat Satan in the earth.

And there was war in heaven. Michael and his angels
fought against the dragon, and the dragon and his angels
fought back. But he was not strong enough, and they lost
their place in heaven. The great dragon was hurled
down–that ancient serpent called the devil or Satan, who
leads the whole world astray. He was hurled to the earth,
and his angels with him. Then I heard a loud voice in
heaven say: 'Now have come the salvation, and the power
and the kingdom of our God, and the authority of his
Christ. For the accuser of our brothers, who accuses them

before God day and night, has been hurled down. THEY
OVERCAME HIM BY THE BLOOD OF THE LAMB AND
BY THE WORD OF THEIR TESTIMONY: they did not
love their lives so much as to shrink from death.
(Revelation 12:7-11) (Emphasis mine.)

Today the devil is attacking the inhabitants of the earth and making war against the saints, those who obey God's commandments and hold to the testimony of Jesus (see Revelation 12:17).

We have known more about *war on the saints* than we have known about *the saints at war.* It is in God's timing for the Church to take the offensive and prevail against the gates of Hades.

VII

The Saints At War

Is spiritual warfare really effective? Can we really change things here on earth by binding the principalities and powers in the heavenlies?

Ruler Spirits Over Churches

In 1974 the Lord relocated me in ministry from Colorado to Texas. In a small Texas community I worked with another pastor who had started the church five years previously. The church was not growing. Three-fourths of the congregation had left, and visitors in Sunday services were rare. Rumors were widespread throughout the community that we worshipped the devil, and people were afraid of us. The outreach of the church was not merely hindered, it was completely bound.

As we prayed about what to do, we were led to give ourselves to prayer and spiritual warfare. We two pastors spent five mornings each week in spiritual battle. For at least four hours each day we would bind the spirits of lying, gossip, hindrance, fear and religious traditionalism which were hindering new people from coming. We saw our efforts as wrestling against the spiritual powers arraigned against us in the heavenlies. A week went by and there was no visible result, yet we knew in our hearts that the pressure on the enemy was mounting. A month went by and still there was no evidence of change, but we were not discouraged. The Holy Spirit was giving us a tenacity in spiritual warfare.

After six weeks there was a dramatic change. A woman who had been deep into witchcraft and sin, and who was at the point of suicide, was saved and delivered from evil spirits. She began to boldly testify to others and brought scores of persons to church. The hindrances were broken and the church began to grow.

The Lord has led me into many experiences of deliverance and spiritual warfare in order to learn from those experiences. I was learning that when a church is hindered in growth and effectiveness, unable to fulfill the ministry to which God called it, the root problem is demonic.

Ruler Spirits Over Geo-Political Areas

A short while later the Lord drew our attention to the crime in our county. The local newspaper was continually reporting the robberies, burglaries, rapes and homicides. Surely these crimes were promoted by Satan. Did we not have the power to bind him?

By this time, we had a group of eight or ten men who met at the church house three hours before service time on Sunday mornings. This group of men took up the challenge of spiritual warfare, and they bound the spirits of crime over our county. The pressure was kept upon these spirits week after week. Several months later the local newspaper gave a report of crime statistics. Each category of crime was lower than previously. Six months later another crime report was given, and the statistics were even lower. There was an editorial in the paper calling attention to the lower crime rate and seeking some logical explanation. It was noted that adjacent counties reported a continued rise in crime in contrast to the lower rates in our own county. Local law enforcement agencies were taking credit for doing an exceptionally good job, but we knew the real cause of the change was due to our binding the strong man of crime in the heavenlies.

Ruler Spirits Over Ethnic Groups

One morning as our men's group was in prayer and spiritual warfare, the Holy Spirit impressed me that we should bind the demonic powers over the Mexican American people in our city. This ethnic group comprised about half of the population of the city, but they were not being reached by the Gospel, and the outpouring of the Holy Spirit had seemingly bypassed them. Why should they not be reached for the Lord?

So we began to bind the spirits of racial and religious prejudice which held these Spanish speaking people in bondage. At the very next service in our church six Spanish speaking people came. They could not understand much of the service because everything was in English, but they kept smiling and enjoying the presence of the Lord. We knew that these people needed to be ministered to in the Spanish language.

The Lord led us to invite a Spanish speaking minister for a special crusade. Over a hundred persons were reached. Many were saved, baptized in the Holy Spirit, healed and delivered of evil spirits. As a follow-up, special services were provided in Spanish for these people, and our church was given a strategic role in ministering to this ethnic group within our city. The door to ministry among these people was opened through warfare in the heavenlies.

Ruler Spirits Over Denominations

In 1979 my wife and I were ministering in Sweden. The young minister and his wife who were hosting us were excited about a reconciliation meeting within their denomination. They told us that several years previously there had been a terrible split among the Pentecostal churches; but, gradually, many of the pastors had been reconciled, and they were bringing their congregations together in the central church in Stockholm for a reconciliation meeting.

A few days before this meeting was held, we were ministering in the church of a pastor who had been directly involved in the division within the denomination. He shared with us how that he and several other ministers had been led to do spiritual warfare. The church building, in which actual fisticuffs had taken place between some of the people, had formerly been used as a prison. The Holy Spirit had revealed to these men that the spirits of strife, rebellion, division and violence were still in the building. They marched around the building (at this point they were not welcomed into the building) binding the spiritual powers in operation there. After this, they began to experience a degree of restored fellowship and were able to go into the building and command the evil spirits to leave. Now the reconciliation of all of the involved congregations was taking place.

As we approached the building to attend this momentous meeting, we were with a young minister and his wife. The minister's wife had been in that church and had witnessed the fighting among the people that had taken place several years previously. Suddenly she froze as though her feet were planted in the cement. She began to tremble and to cry. The thought of going back into that building terrified her. We prayed for her right there on the street and cast out spirits of fear. Then she was able to go in to the meeting.

It was a very emotionally-packed occasion as we witnessed the healing of relationships within a denomination. The key to this restoration of fellowship was the direct result of spiritual warfare and prayer. The principalities and powers that had created the division had been bound. Satan's kingdom was defeated: and the Kingdom of God, a kingdom of righteousness, peace and joy in the Holy Ghost, prevailed.

Ruler Spirits Over Geographical Territories

In the winter of 1982 the Lord sent us to the icy wilderness of the Yukon Territory in northwestern Canada. The small fellowship that invited us was zealous to witness, but was discouraged from lack of results. It had been a long time since anyone had been brought to Christ through their ministry. We taught them the message given in this book. About twelve members began to meet an hour before the service each evening for prayer and spiritual warfare. We bound the spirits over the Yukon. At the first prayer meeting, the Lord revealed to me the strong spirits over the Yukon Territory. The ruler spirit was called "Wilderness." His helpers were escapism, loneliness, alcoholism, wickedness, hardness, indifference, cruelty, covetousness, greed, pride, prejudice (racial, religious and territorial), independence, rebellion, deception, sexual perverseness and generation curses from the heathen practices of the Indians. The discernment of the "Wilderness" spirit was confirmed a few days later when we visited a museum. There was a relief map of the Territory showing an ice wilderness out of which several glaciers flowed. The ice is said to be one and a half miles deep. There are two high mountains located within this wilderness of Kluana. The area around these twin peaks was called "The Holy of Holies of Kluana," a counterfeit of God's sanctuary, and the headquarters of the wilderness spirit.

After a few days of spiritual warfare, there was a definite breakthrough in the ministry. Several persons came on their own initiative to seek salvation. These people came to the meetings saying they needed to know how to become saved. While meeting on a small Indian reservation, a woman came to the meeting who had driven 100 miles over the Al-Can Highway in a temperature of 60 degrees below zero. She announced that she had heard of the meeting and had come to give her heart to Jesus.

Nine months later the pastor wrote me to report that a definite change had taken place in the ministry since they began to bind the strong man. Growth and spiritual fruit was still being experienced. He said there was even a different atmosphere over the Territory, and people were wondering what had happened to the Yukon.

Ruler Spirits Over Nations

ENGLAND

Our first ministry in England was in 1979. We found very little emphasis upon deliverance and spiritual warfare. One precious brother, a retired British Naval Captain, and his lovely wife were very active in deliverance ministry, but they knew of only a few others working in deliverance.

Spiritual warfare against the principalities and powers over England was emphasized in our teachings. We found in England strong powers of witchcraft, spiritism and occultism that went back past the first century from the influence of the ancient Druids. There were strong powers of dead, traditional religion *having a form of godliness but denying the power of it* (II Timothy 3:5).

We were told that about two percent of the people in England attended church, and 90 percent regularly consulted occult sources for knowledge, guidance and power.

When we returned to England in 1983, we found an improved spiritual atmosphere. In a month's time we ministered in 18 churches, all of whom were much involved in deliverance and zealous for spiritual warfare. We met a group of Christians dedicated to spiritual warfare who were focusing their warfare against the ancient Druid spirits. They were visiting the sites of old Druid temples and binding the spirits associated with them. The history of witchcraft in England goes back to the Druids who lived in England at the time of Christ. Later, Anglican churches were built on the sites of some of the old Druid temples. The group reported that spiritual awakening was coming to these Anglican churches and to the areas where the ruler spirits were bound. We could readily see the effectiveness of spiritual warfare since the saints had begun to bind the strong man over England.

In 1984 we returned to England. This time we met with 120 pastors and church leaders for a five-day conference on spiritual warfare. There was an unusually strong anointing of the Holy Spirit on these meetings. The pastors were enthusiastic about the teachings on spiritual warfare, and they are being faithful to press the battle against the demonic powers over the nation of England. We are encouraged to see the army of the Lord coming forth in Great Britain. The warfare has just begun, but the ground already gained is encouraging.

KOREA

A country where the strong man has already been bound for several years is South Korea. In the summer of 1984 I attended a conference where Paul Yonggi Cho, pastor of a church in Korea that is experiencing phenomenal growth, was sharing with pastors and church leaders. He said people wanted to know the secret of the successful church growth in Korea where 10,000 people are being added to the church each month.

Pastor Cho said. "We just pray and obey." Thousands of People in Korea are zealous in prayer. There is a place called "Prayer Mountain" where these thousands go to pray each day. Cho explained that through such praying the powers over Korea have been bound, and the Kingdom of God is expanding.

Pastor Cho told us about an American army chaplain who was having a very successful ministry in Korea among the American service men. The chaplain could not understand the mighty move of God through his ministry. The chaplain had previously been stationed in West Germany where he preached the same sermons with little success. Why would there be such a fruitful ministry in Korea? Cho explained to him that Satan's principalities over Korea had been bound, and that anyone with a Gospel ministry could be successful in Korea.

FRANCE

In 1985 my wife and I received our first invitation to lead a deliverance conference in France. Our excitement over this new door of opportunity was tempered by preliminary reports of strong resistance in France to the message of spiritual warfare. Pastor John Edwards of Croydon, England, our frequent co-worker in European ministries, preceded us into France with two preliminary deliverance conferences in which to "test the waters."

Pastor Edwards discerned the satanic powers of resistance in France. Therefore, weeks in advance of our conference, he called his church to spiritual warfare against the ruler spirits over France. Each weekday morning up to fifty members of the Croydon church met to pray for the meetings in France and to bind the hindering spirits. Then, fifty intercessors from the Croydon church went by chartered bus to France in support of the conference.

The results from the spiritual warfare were obvious. There was a large attendance and a powerful anointing for deliverance. All resistance was gone. The people came, entered in and received from God.

The Holy Spirit even opened another door of opportunity. I was invited to be a speaker at the French national convention of the Full Gospel Business Men's Fellowship International. Deliverance was a major emphasis at this convention. I was free to teach and minister deliverance to hundreds of people. At least twelve countries were represented among those attending.

The door which God opened into France was great and effectual. The many adversaries were bound. Our prayers were answered. A strong deposit of deliverance influence was left in France. Once again we experienced a fruitful

71

ministry as the combined result of intercessory prayer and spiritual warfare.

BRAZIL/URUGUAY

A modern illustration revealing the influence of strongholds in geographical areas comes from a story that appeared in a magazine called *'Acts'* published by the World Map organization:

"A missionary was working in a new area in the mountains of Brazil and Uruguay in South America. He was witnessing in a village situated directly on the border of the two nations. In fact, the border ran down the center of main street. He was distributing Gospel tracts during a shopping day when he noticed something quite unusual.

"On the Uruguayan side of the main street, no one would accept his Gospel tracts. But, on the Brazilian side, everyone accepted the tracts graciously, and were open to hearing his testimony concerning his faith in Christ. He moved back and forth across the street with the same bewildering results. Then he noticed a woman who had refused his tract on the Uruguayan side of the street cross to the Brazilian side. He followed her and again offered her a tract. She accepted it gratefully, and he was able to witness to her about the Lord.

"The missionary realized something very strange was going on. He began checking with other missionaries and believers in that particular area of Brazil. He discovered there was a group of Christians who had entered into spiritual warfare. They were involved in intercessory prayer, and had literally taken authority over and bound the prince in that area of Brazil.

"Wherever the Gospel was preached there, tremendous

revival was occurring. But the awesome realization that shook the missionary was the fact that the revival ended at the geographical boundary; the stronghold over that area of Brazil ended at the border in the center of main street."[1]

The Call Goes Out

Then the Spirit of the Lord came upon Gideon, and he blew a trumpet. (Judges 6:34)

Gideon had been called of God and sent to deliver Israel out of the hand of the Midianites who had introduced Baal worship among God's people. Even Gideon's own father had erected an altar of Baal and an idolatrous Asherah pole beside it. Gideon's first move was to take his father's young bullock and tear down the heathen worship center. Thus, Gideon attacked the strong man over Israel which was Baal worship. Then, under the Lord's instructions, he blew a trumpet and summoned others to join him in the battle against the Midianites. Thirty-two thousand men responded, but when God weeded out the fearful and the uncommitted only 300 remained. God used Gideon's 300 men to defeat the Midianites: and they did so with some very peculiar weapons: trumpets, pitchers, torches and shouting.

Today God has raised up a Gideon company to lead the way into spiritual warfare. It is attacking the strong men over every aspect of Satan's Kingdom. It is blowing the

---

[1] *The Power of Praise and Worship* by Terry Law, P. 46-47, Victory House Publishers, Tulsa, Oklahoma, 1985.

Lord's trumpet summoning others to join the ranks in spiritual battle. God is not impressed with numbers, but God will use a band of committed soldiers to defeat the rulers, authorities, powers of this dark world and the spiritual forces of evil in the heavenly realm (see Ephesians 6:12). They will win the victory by using the strange weapons that God has given them.

> *For though we live in the world, we do not wage war as the world does. The weapons we fight with are not the weapons of the world. On the contrary, they have divine power to demolish strongholds.*
>
> (II Corinthians 10:3-4)

VIII

The Saints At War
(Continued)

There are practical questions which come to mind concerning spiritual warfare: How does one know the name of the strong man over an area? How is he bound? Who should bind him? How long does it take to bind him? How long does he stay bound? Some of these questions do not have absolute answers. Most of the time we do not need absolute answers. We are prone to forget that the Holy Spirit is given to us as our Guide. Instead of looking for pat answers and methods, we must develop a dependence upon the Holy Spirit to enlighten and instruct us in spiritual battle. We do not follow methods; we follow the Holy Spirit.

Identifying The Strong Man

One of the gifts of the Holy Spirit is *discerning of spirits* (I Corinthians 12:10, KJV). Through the operation of this gift, the presence and nature of evil spirits are determined. This is a supernatural way of knowing and distinguishing what is before you in the spirit realm. Through prayer, I ask the Holy Spirit to reveal to me the nature of the strong man over whatever situation I am confronting.

When we were learning the principles of spiritual warfare, we were living in the mountains of Colorado. In a vision the Lord revealed to my wife the strong man over our county. She saw a large, black octopus suspended over the mountains where we lived. Across his forehead was written the word "Jealousy." That was the name of the strong man. Each of his eight tentacles bore names: selfishness, pride, contention, envy, suspicion, covetousness, greed and division. These eight spirits were the strong man's helpers. In the vision the tentacles were wrapped around each area of community life: church, business, school, government and recreation. This was an accurate picture of what we actually saw happening in our community. The revealing of the strong man over the area was given by the Holy Spirit through the gift of discerning of spirits.

In other instances, the nature of the strong man is known by observing what he is doing. What evil is pre-dominant? This is a key to determining the identity of the strong man. Watch for a prevailing problem. Is it mental illness, alcoholism, divorce, adultery, religious exclusiveness, or what?

Use whatever insight you have, whether by discernment or detection, and begin to utilize your understanding in spiritual warfare. Usually, as you initiate a warfare the Lord will reveal more to you.

Awareness of Hindrances

Sometimes when I am ministering in a country or city where I have not been previously, there will be spiritual hindrances in the meetings. I may have no liberty in preaching, and the people may be hindered in hearing what is taught. Both of these hindrances manifested themselves when we made our first trip to Sweden.

We had been ministering in Denmark three weeks before we went to Sweden. There was freedom in the meetings in Denmark, but we hit resistance when we entered Sweden. It was our first trip to Europe; and the Spirit was teaching us that, when we go from one nation to another, we come under different ruler spirits, and we must be prepared for them.

When we encountered the resistance, we stopped teaching and led the congregation in spiritual warfare to bind the strong man over Sweden. As we prayed, it was revealed to us that the strong man was "Liberation." The goal in Sweden seems to be complete liberation of everything. The human body is liberated through nudity and sexual lust. Even incest has been legalized. Women are liberated through independence and anti-submissiveness. Many of them are lascivious in dress and behavior. If an unwanted pregnancy occurs, abortion is the solution. Couples are liberated from the marriage covenant through common law marriage (fornication) and through divorce. Children are liberated from punishment. It is illegal for parents to spank a child without the permission of the child.

The hindrance in our meeting was the liberation of the mind. A prevailing philosophy in Sweden is that one does not have to either agree or disagree with what he hears. This attitude results in passivity of the mind. So, as I taught the Word, no one was seeking to relate to the truth. After thirty minutes of spiritual warfare, the spirit of liberation was bound, and thereafter the gospel had free course.

The Power of Praise

Praise is a weapon of warfare. It can be used to bind demonic strong men.

> *Let the saints rejoice in this honor and sing for joy on their beds. May the praise of God be in their mouths and a double-edged sword in their hands, to inflict vengeance on the nations and punishment on the peoples, to bind their kings with fetters, their nobles with shackles of iron, to carry out the sentence written against them. This is the glory of all his saints.* (Psalm 149:5-9)

I am reminded of a time when we experienced the binding power of the high praises of God. We were in church in a certain state, and the Holy Spirit led us into the heights of praise. The entire congregation was swept up in the praise. We marched, sang and shouted unto the Lord. At the height of the praises, the Holy Spirit spoke through a word of knowledge (I Corinthians 12:8) that through our praise we were binding the strong man over that state. While the instruments continued the praise, the congregation took authority over the state's strong man. After fifteen minutes of warfare, we knew the strong man was bound. In the next gubernatorial election a corrupt governor was removed from office.

Our warfare is not against *flesh and blood*. However, ruler spirits work through men. When the ruler spirits are thrown down, the men through whom they work are also toppled. An illustration of this principle is found in Acts where King Herod was used of the devil to persecute the Church. He had killed James and Peter was imprisoned. The Church was praying earnestly. Their prayers brought angelic intervention, and Peter was supernaturally released

78

from prison. Then judgment was brought upon Herod and *an angel of the Lord struck him down. and he was eaten by worms and died* (Acts 32:23).

The Church did not organize a protest, march on the king's palace, boobytrap the king's chariot or bribe anyone. They prayed earnestly. For *the prayer of a righteous man is powerful and effective* (James 5:16).

It is such a temptation to employ fleshly tactics instead of directing the warfare toward the satanic powers controlling men. Our tactics must not be fleshly. For example, the way to combat the problem of abortion is not to burn and bomb abortion clinics. The problem of abortion is caused by sin in man's heart fostered by Satan's lies. The same is true of the spreading cancer of homosexuality.

Men are used as Satan's pawns to foster Satan worship, sexual perverseness, murder by abortion, drug traffic, alcoholism and crime. Much effort is expended today in combatting these sorts of problems as merely sociological in nature rather than demonic. Men are attacked or made objects of social reform, and the devil escapes unchallenged.

Religious Strong Men

Wherever we have gone in the United States or abroad, we have always found strong religious spirits. The devil promotes religiosity. The Pharisees were extremely religious, but Jesus said they were of their father, the devil. Religious spirits promote division, religious pride, false doctrines, damnable heresies and idolatry. Such spirits bring many curses upon peoples and even upon entire nations.

On a trip to South America we encountered false

religious spirits in full bloom. A spirit of religious control holds the republic of Colombia in its grasp. Its idolatry is displayed from the lowest valley to the highest mountain. This religious spirit parades itself as "Christian," but it is a crude mixture of biblical terminology, human tradition and heathen superstition.

Witchcraft, spiritism and every form of occultism are found in Colombia. These practices are forms of false religion. On one of Colombia's islands the "in thing" was found to be charms. Most of the people in the church services were laden with 18-carat gold bracelets and necklaces filled with golden charms. Witches and mediums were discovered in some of the crusade meetings. Some were saved and delivered of evil spirits.

There is a move of God in South America. It was obvious to us that the most effective work was being done by those who were involved in spiritual warfare and deliverance. There is an army of true believers who are binding the strong men who have held multitudes in vain religion, poverty and sickness. Thousands are repenting of their sins and embracing Jesus Christ as Savior and Lord.

The Cloud of Communism

On a trip via automobile into Poland we crossed communist Czechoslovakia. Anyone sensitive to the spirit realm could sense the spiritual greyness and oppression that hung over that country like a cloud. We experienced the same thing when we crossed into Poland. The absence of joy was stifling. The people in the services could not lift their heads, could not look us in the eyes and could not enter into praise. They were unable to receive salvation, healing or deliverance. They were immobilized by oppression.

The battle against the strong man of Communism took a unique approach. I awoke the morning after our arrival in Poland to the shrill sound of my wife's voice. The sound was coming from the balcony just outside our bedroom on the third floor. I sat up with a start. She was shouting the word, "joy," as loudly as she could, and the sound was echoing across the mountainside. I went to the door and inquired, "What are you doing?" She explained that during the night the Holy Spirit had instructed her that when she arose she was to go outside and shout "joy" to the land. It really caused a stir, because no one else in the building understood English, and everyone came outside to see if the house was on fire.

Later that morning our host pastor took us for a hike up the mountain. We hiked along a beautiful, clear stream of water. The pastor explained to us that the stream was the headwaters of the Vistula River which flowed all the way across Poland. The Lord spoke to Ida Mae's heart that we should speak "joy" into the stream, and that it would be a symbol of God's joy spreading across the entire country. It seemed more appropriate to speak joy in Polish, so the pastor taught us to pronounce their word for joy, *radosc*, and we shouted it into the river.

We continued to speak *radosc* to the land every day. For the first three days there was no response in the meetings. The heaviness hung in the air like a grey mist. Then on the fourth night there was a breakthrough. People began to come forward. Some came to receive salvation, and other came to receive healing. A dozen were baptized in the Holy Spirit. Then the praise broke forth, and we could see their smiling faces. Hands were being lifted up to the Lord, and people were singing. A few even danced unto the

Lord. Cameras were clicking to record the breakthrough. It was a glorious time. The strong man of heaviness had been bound, and the people had put on their garments of praise (see Isaiah 61:3).

There, in the south of Poland, at the headwaters of the Vistula River, the trickle of joy began to flow through the hearts of a few people for whom Christ died. The spiritual battle is underway. They are not fighting men, nor political system, but they are fighting against the power of Satan. Satan has destroyed the joy and peace, which are the rightful blessings of God's people. We did not teach them to defy their government, but to wage war in the heavenlies.

Questions, Questions

Who should bind the strong men? Christ gave the "keys" of Kingdom authority to His Church. Therefore, the greatest application of this authority over Satan comes when the Church stands in unity against him. Those to whom Christ has given delegated authority in the Church and in the family should exercise their spiritual authority in binding the strong men. Individuals should bind the strong men as the Spirit leads.

How long does it take to bind a strong man? In the natural some men are stronger than others. The same is true in the spiritual realm. Jesus said concerning certain demons. *This kind goeth not out but by prayer and fasting* (Matthew 17:21. KJV). Some kinds of demons are stronger and more determined than others. Our warfare against them is termed wrestling (see Ephesians 6:12). A wrestling victory is achieved by putting superior pressure on one's opponent until he is pinned.

This is an accurate picture of our warfare. The devil has put pressure on us, but now the saints are putting the pressure on him, and we maintain that pressure until he is immobilized–bound! This defeat may take anywhere from a few seconds to a few months.

How does one know when the strong man is bound? When he is bound you will see the results, and you will know it in your own heart.

How long does the strong man remain bound? As long as you keep him bound. He will be like a man struggling at the ropes that bind him until he wiggles loose. Our spiritual lives should be consistent, not hit and miss. As we remain steadfast in prayer and spiritual warfare, we will keep the ropes tight, and the strong man will remain bound.

IX

Beginning at Jerusalem

Where do God's saints begin in their spiritual battle to conquer the world for Christ, and to bring the Kingdom of God on earth? Jesus set the pattern for us when He commissioned His Church to take the Gospel into all the world. He said:

> *And you shall be my witnesses in Jerusalem, and in all Judea and Samaria, and unto the ends of the earth.*
> (Acts 1:8)

Jerusalem was the location of the temple, the place where God's presence resided. Jerusalem speaks of the Christian whose body is now *the temple of the Holy Spirit, who is in you* (I Corinthians 6:19). The first place to cleanse and conquer is in one's own life.

When Jesus entered the temple in Jerusalem He found it defiled. Therefore, the glory of God was having to indwell a defiled temple. Jesus was moved with righteous indignation. He cleansed the temple by casting out the cattle, doves and money changers. Today each believer is God's temple, His dwelling place. Does God's Holy Spirit live amidst defilement? Are there unclean things in the outer court of one's life? Is the mind filled with unclean thoughts? Are the members of one's body yielded to gluttony or fornication? Do fear, anxiety and worry rule the emotions?

The Christian soldier will be hindered in spiritual warfare until his own life is free. Your "Jerusalem," your own life, must become the palace of King Jesus. He must reign as Lord over every area of your being. If anything else is enthroned it must be seen as an enemy and war declared against it. Kingdom life will become a reality to you when everything pertaining to Satan is removed and Jesus rules as Lord of all.

Judea

Judea is the next logical area of conquest. The people of Judea were all of one family. Satan and his demons are in control of many families, or at least of certain members within those families. This is grounds for a declaration of war against the enemy of the home.

Don't be afraid of them. Remember the Lord, who is great and awesome, and fight for your brothers. your sons and your daughters, your wives and your homes.
(Nehemiah 4:14)

Judea was also a nation, composed of cities and villages. The Christian soldier must fight to free his city and his nation from demonic powers. The nature of such "principalities and powers" can usually be determined by observing the evil conditions existing within a given geopolitical area. Through prayer, the Holy Spirit will reveal the specific "strong man" and his helpers which must be bound. The English word "principality" is defined by Webster as "the territory or jurisdiction of a prince." Satan has assigned delegated demonic princes to rule over each segment of our nation. The Christian warriors in each city and community should assume responsibility for binding

Satan's princes (strong men). The Church within a given nation should bear responsibility for the spiritual warfare in behalf of that nation. Then, in a broader application, the universal body of Christ should battle with and for one another throughout the world.

Samaria

In the story of The Good Samaritan, Jesus taught that Samaria represents one's neighbor. That neighbor can be a person who lives in your neighborhood, or who lives in a neighboring geographical territory. The important thing to comprehend is the expanding dimensions of our spiritual warfare from self, to family, and then to one's neighbors. The man who fell among thieves needed a good neighbor. The good Samaritan who aided him was different from those who passed by him. He could help his neighbor because he was free from racial and religious prejudices as well as free from selfishness. He had compassion on the wounded man whom the thief had robbed and almost killed. Jesus would have us exhibit the same compassionate help towards those whom Satan has assaulted.

Sometimes our neighbors, whether persons across the street or nations across the ocean, become our enemies. They pose threats to our security and peace. They are influenced or even controlled by Satan, the deceiver. Rather than warring against flesh and blood, which is a strong temptation amid such circumstances, we must learn to bind the ruler spirits involved.

The Ends of the Earth

Our spiritual warfare will eventually embrace the whole

world. Jesus Christ, our Commander in Chief, is leading His army today into spiritual world conquest. The devil is not ignorant of this fact, and that is why we see such bold and desperate moves on his part to stir up every trouble imaginable. *Because the devil has gone down to you! He is filled with fury, because he knows that his time is short* (Revelation 12:12).

The Trumpet Sound

When you go into battle in your own land against an enemy who is oppressing you, sound a blast on the trumpets. Then you will be remembered by the Lord your God and rescued from your enemies.

(Numbers 10:9)

The trumpets are sounding today! The summons is universal. Each Christian in every nation of the world is called to battle. It is time to be diligent and specific. Identify Satan's forces in the heavenlies, and wrestle them until they are bound.

A Deliverance Prayer

Lord Jesus Christ, I believe that You are the Son of God. You came in the flesh, lived without sin, died a substitutionary death upon the cross for my sins and rose from the grave on the third day.

You redeemed me by Your blood and I belong to You. It is my desire to live for You and to glorify Your name. I confess all of my sins, known and unknown, and I ask You to forgive me. Forgive me now and cleanse me with Your blood. I forgive all others as I want You to forgive me.

You know my special needs: the things that hinder, that torment and that defile. I come to You as my Deliverer. I claim the promise of Your Word, **"And everyone who calls on the name of the Lord will be saved, for...there will be deliverance as the Lord has said"** *(Joel 2:32). I call upon You now. In the name of the Lord Jesus Christ, deliver me and set me free. Amen.*

A Warfare Declaration

Note: The following is an example of how to command Satan and his evil spirits:

Satan, I come against you in the name of my Lord Jesus Christ. I am His child, redeemed by His blood. I have repented of all my sins and have received God's forgiveness. In obedience to God's command, I have forgiven each person who has ever trespassed against me and all for whom I have held resentment.

I have confessed the sins of my ancestors, and have renounced every inherited curse. I take back from you all the ground that you ever gained in my life. You have no rights of dominion over me. Jesus has given me authority to bind you and to cast you out, and you cannot harm me. All of your plans against me are frustrated and cancelled. Every strong man assigned against me is bound.

I command every evil spirit which has gained entrance to me to leave me now in the mighty name of Jesus. (Press the battle until you are free).

Note: Personalize specific things that you recognize (or even suspect) to be attacks of demons against you, your family, your church, your community, your nation and other nations.

Make your personal list of evil spirits to be bound. Then pray a deliverance prayer, and make your declaration against Satan.

They overcame him by the blood of the lamb
and by the word of their testimony.
(Revelation 12:11)

Demons Attacking My Own Life

REJECTION LONER FORGET OUTCAST
NOT FITTING IN,

Demons Attacking My Family

DAD DEMENTIA ALZ FORGET CURSEING ANGER
MOM REJECTION FORGET FORGIVENESS
RAGE, HATE,

Demons Attacking The Church

Demons Attacking My City Or Community

Demons Attacking My Nation

Demons Attacking Other Nations

CERDOS EN LA SALA

More than 500,000 copies of PIGS IN THE PARLOR, the recognized handbook of Deliverance, are continuing to help set people free around the world from demonic bondages. This Bestseller is now also available IN SPANISH — at the same price as the English edition.

Paperback 5.95

KINGDOM LIVING FOR THE FAMILY

A long awaited sequel to PIGS IN THE PARLOR, offering not mere unrealistic theories, but rather a Practical Plan for implementing divine order in the family, and preventing the need for deliverance.

Paperback 5.95

OVERCOMING REJECTION

Powerful help for confronting and dealing with rejection, which so often is found to be a root in individuals requiring deliverance. This book will help understand a tool commonly employed by the enemy in his attacks upon believers.

Paperback 5.95

IMPACT CHRISTIAN BOOKS, INC.
Announces

The Exciting New Power for Deliverance Series:

Power for Deliverance; Songs of Deliverance
Power for Deliverance From Fat
Power for Deliverance for Children
Power for Deliverance From Childlessness

Lives have already been changed by the powerful truths and revelations contained in these books as the author has taught them over the past seventeen years. These deliverance tools have been tested in the crucible of prayer room battles to free lives from Satan's control. You have tasted in this book the kind of dramatic accounts and truths which are to be found in the other volumes in this series.

Each book is just $5.95. When ordering, add $1.50 postage and handling for the first book and $.50 for each additional title.

Available at your local Christian bookstore, library,
or directly from:

Impact Christian Books, Inc.
332 Leffingwell Avenue, Suite 101
Kirkwood, MO 63122

The
Acts
of
Pilate

ANCIENT RECORDS RECORDED BY
CONTEMPORARIES OF JESUS CHRIST
REGARDING THE FACTS CONCERNING
HIS BIRTH, DEATH, RESURRECTION

♦

TRANSLATED FROM THE ORIGINAL LANGUAGES
BY DRS, MCINTOSH and TWYMAN

♦

EDITED BY REV. W.D. MAHAN

This book was a favorite of the late Kathryn Kuhlman who often read from it on her radio show.

Early Church Writers such as Justin refer to the existence of these records, and Tertullian specifically mentions the report made by Pilate to the Emperor of Rome, Tiberius Caesar.

Chapters Include:
♦ *How These Records Were Discovered,*
♦ *A Short Sketch of the Talmuds,*
♦ *Constantine's Letter in Regard to Having Fifty Copies of the Scriptures Written and Bound,*
♦ *Jonathan's Interview with the Bethlehem Shepherds   Letter of Melker, Priest of the Synagogue at Bethlehem,*
♦ *Gamaliel's Interview with Joseph and Mary and Others Concerning Jesus,*
♦ *Report of Caiaphas to the Sanhedrim Concerning the Resurrection of Jesus,*
♦ *Valleus's Notes — "Acta Pilati," or Pilate's Report to Caesar of the Arrest, Trial, and Crucifixion of Jesus,*
♦ *Herod Antipater's Defense Before the Roman Senate in Regard to His Conduct At Bethlehem,*
♦ *Herod Antipas's Defense Before the Roman Senate in Regard to the Execution of John the Baptist,*
♦ *The Hillel Letters Regarding God's Providence to the Jews, by Hillel the Third*

THE ACTS OF PILATE $9.95, plus $2.00 Shipping

IMPACT CHRISTIAN BOOKS, INC.
332 Leffingwell Ave., Suite 101, Kirkwood, MO 63122

FOR ADDITIONAL COPIES WRITE:

Impac Christian Books

332 Leffingwell Ave., Suite 101
Kirkwood, MO 63122

AVAILABLE AT YOUR LOCAL BOOKSTORE, OR YOU MAY
ORDER DIRECTLY. Toll-Free, order-line only M/C, DISC,
or VISA 1-800-451-2708.